WHY DO I POO?

BY Kirsty Holmes

Published in 2019 by Crabtree Publishing Company

First Published by Book Life in 2018
Copyright © 2018 Book Life

Printed in the U.S.A./082018/CG20180601

Published in Canada
Crabtree Publishing
616 Welland Avenue
St. Catharines, ON
L2M 5V6

Published in the United States
Crabtree Publishing
PMB 59051
350 Fifth Ave, 59th Floor
New York, NY 10118

Author: Kirsty Holmes

Editors: Holly Duhig, Kathy Middleton

Design: Danielle Rippengill

Proofreader: Janine Deschenes

Prepress technician: Samara Parent

Print coordinator: Katharine Berti

All facts, statistics, web addresses and URLs in this book were verified as valid and accurate at time of writing. No responsibility for any changes to external websites or references can be accepted by either the author or publisher.

Photographs

All images are courtesy of Shutterstock.com, unless otherwise specified. With thanks to Getty Images, Thinkstock Photo and iStockphoto. Front Cover & 1 – Dmitry Natashin, Nadzin, MaryValery, zizi_mentos, HedgehogVector. Images used on every spread – Nadzin, TheFarAwayKingdom. 2 – zizi_mentos, anpannan. 4 – Iconic Bestiary, zizi_mentos, HedgehogVector. 5 – zizi_mentos, anpannan. 6 & 7 – Vector Tradition SM. 8 & 9 – TheFarAwayKingdom. 9 – Ienjoyeverytime. 10 & 11 – LOVE YOU, momojung, anpannan, zizi_mentos. 12 – light_s. 13 – zizi_mentos, Jakkarin chuenaka, robuart, Sunflowerr, KlaraD, Panda Vector. 14 – Maike Hildebrandt, Mr. Luck, HedgehogVector. 15 – Iconic Bestiary, 32. 16 – svtdesign, anpannan. 17 – LANTERIA, HedgehogVector. 18 & 19 – tenmami. 20 – marysuperstudio, Colorcocktail, zizi_mentos, CW design luncher, Maksim M. 21 – alazur, graphicrepublic, zizi_mentos. 22 – Beatriz Gascon J, benchart, johavel. 23 – Nadya_Art, Studio_G, Sudowoodo.

Library and Archives Canada Cataloguing in Publication

Holmes, Kirsty Louise, author
        Why do I poo? / Kirsty Holmes.

(Why do I?)
Includes index.
Issued in print and electronic formats.
ISBN 978-0-7787-5144-1 (hardcover).--
ISBN 978-0-7787-5150-2 (softcover).--
ISBN 978-1-4271-2174-5 (HTML)

        1. Feces--Juvenile literature. 2. Excretion--Juvenile literature.
3. Digestion--Juvenile literature. 4. Digestive organs--Juvenile literature.
5. Human physiology--Juvenile literature. I. Title.

QP159.H65 2018   j612.3'6   C2018-902402-X
                                              C2018-902403-8

Library of Congress Cataloging-in-Publication Data

Names: Holmes, Kirsty, author.
Title: Why do I poo? / Kirsty Holmes.
Description: New York, New York : Crabtree Publishing Company, 2019. |
Series: Why do I? | Includes index.
Identifiers: LCCN 2018021333 (print) | LCCN 2018021788 (ebook) |
    ISBN 9781427121745 (Electronic) |
    ISBN 9780778751441 (hardcover) |
    ISBN 9780778751502 (pbk.)
Subjects: LCSH: Defecation--Juvenile literature. | Feces--Juvenile literature. |
    Digestion--Juvenile literature. | Human physiology--Juvenile literature.
Classification: LCC QP159 (ebook) | LCC QP159 .H66 2019 (print) |
    DDC 612.3/6--dc23
LC record available at https://lccn.loc.gov/2018021333

CONTENTS

Words that look like **this** can be found in the glossary on page 24.

Do You Need the Bathroom?

Birds do it, bears do it, and mice that live under the stairs do it. Everybody poos! But have you ever wondered why we poo?

Where does poo come from? Where does it go?

You eat and drink every day. Your body takes out what it needs from the food to stay healthy. Then it gets rid of the parts of food it does not need. This is poo and pee!

Food Goes In

All people need to eat. Food gives us nutrients. These are the substances people need to stay alive and healthy. When you eat, different body parts break down food and take out nutrients for your body to use.

Learn more about the parts of your body that break down food on pages 12 and 13.

You need many different nutrients each day. Here is what you get from a spaghetti dinner.

Getting all the right nutrients from food is called having a balanced diet.

MEAT helps build muscles.

TOMATOES give you vitamins **and** minerals.

SPAGHETTI helps give you energy.

MILK helps build bones.

Breaking Down Food

The first stop on food's journey through your body is the mouth. Each of the parts of your mouth do a job to break down food.

Lips keep food inside the mouth.

Front teeth are sharp for biting.

The throat **leads down to your stomach.**

The tongue moves food around in your mouth.

Back teeth are flatter for chewing.

When you eat, the first thing you do is chew your food into smaller pieces. It must be a mushy ball before you can swallow it.

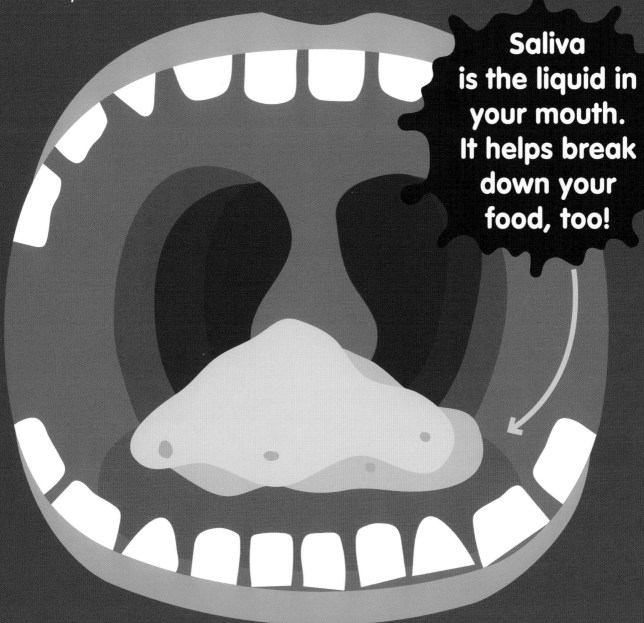

Saliva is the liquid in your mouth. It helps break down your food, too!

After food is swallowed, it moves through your body and different body parts take nutrients out.

Poo Comes Out

HIGH FIBER FOOD

Fiber is the tough parts of food that are hard for your body to break down. Eating foods that have a lot of fiber helps poo come out more easily.

After your body takes all the useful nutrients out of your food, there are usually parts left over. The parts of food your body cannot use are called waste. Waste comes out of you as poo!

Poo is made up mostly of water and fiber. It also contains a slime called **mucus**. Mucus helps poo slide through your body. Poo also contains tiny living things called bacteria.

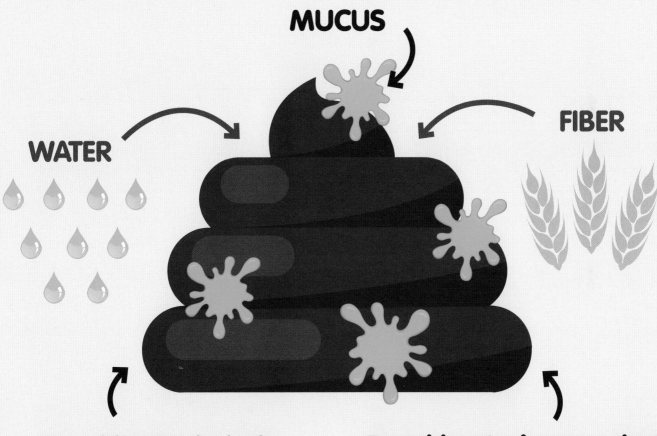

MUCUS

WATER

FIBER

Good bacteria help break down food.

Dead bacteria are what makes your poo smelly!

JOURNEY OF POO

HOW DOES PIZZA BECOME POO?

STEP 1:
Chew up the pizza in your mouth. Then swallow it.

STEP 2:
The chewed pizza travels down a long tube to your **stomach.** Special muscles push and squeeze the food down, like toothpaste through a tube!

STEP 3:
The food sits in your stomach for about 4 hours! A special substance breaks the food down into nutrients your body can use.

STEP 5: The unused parts of the food are squashed into poo, or waste.

STEP 6: Poo leaves your body when you are on the toilet.

STEP 4: The useful nutrients are taken in through the **intestines** and sent to the rest of the body.

Pee And Gas

Poo isn't the only waste your body makes.

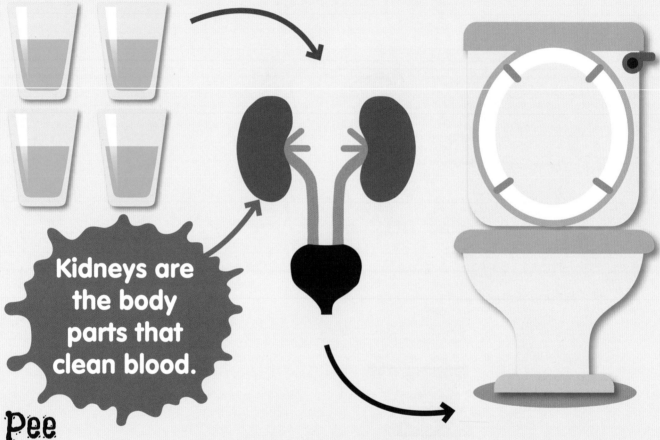

Kidneys are the body parts that clean blood.

Pee

You also make a liquid waste called urine. (That is your pee!) Body parts that clean your blood make pee. Unneeded or harmful things in your blood leave your body in your pee.

Gas

Your body makes gases inside you as it breaks down your food. Gases are substances similar to air. They escape from your body in the same place your poo comes out.

Stomach Pain

It's a poo-mergency!

Sometimes your poo can be very hard or you cannot poo at all. This is called constipation.

Constipation can feel like a stomachache.

Sometimes you might need to go so bad you cannot hold it. If poo comes out watery, this is called diarrhea.

You can get constipation or diarrhea for many reasons. It can happen because of what you eat, how much water you drink, or if you are sick. Tell a parent or caregiver if your poo comes too fast or if you cannot go at all.

Rate Your Poo!

How your poo looks can tell you about your health. Poo comes in different shapes, sizes, and colors. Poo is normally a shade of brown. A red color in your poo could be blood, and means you should tell a parent or caregiver.

1.

Hard, dark pebbles:
Bad constipation
(Tell a parent or caregiver.)

2. **Little lumpy sausage:**
Mild constipation
(Drink more water.)

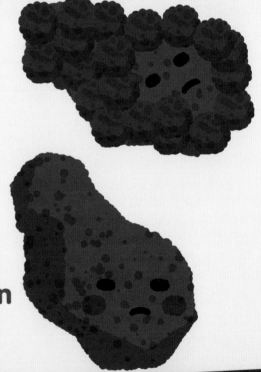

3. **Little cracked sausage:**
First sign of constipation
(Drink more water.)

4. Long, smooth sausage shape: THE PERFECT POO!

Don't touch your poo. Always wash your hands after using the toilet!

5. Soft blob: (Eat more fiber so your poo sticks together.)

7. Liquid: Bad diarrhea (Tell a parent or caregiver.)

6. Mushy: Mild diarrhea (Tell a parent or caregiver.)

Super Poopers!

Poo Power!

Poo gives off a gas that can be burned to make energy, such as electricity, that powers our homes!

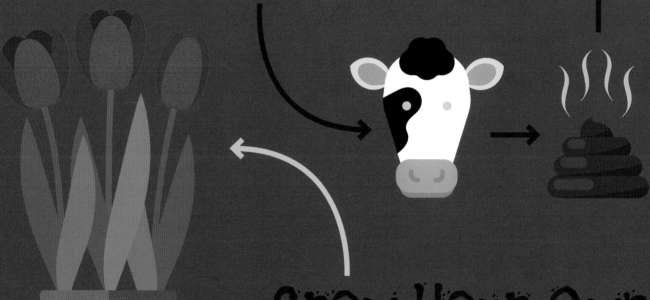

Grow Your Own!

Spreading animal poo on plants helps them grow.

People Power!

In 2014, the first poo-powered bus hit the streets in the United Kingdom. The bus uses energy created by human waste. The bus was given the route number 2. (Get it?)

Poo Paper!

Poo has a lot of fiber in it. So does paper. Some people make paper out of elephant poo, sheep poo, and even panda poo!

Whose Poo?

Can you match the poo to the pooper in this stinky quiz?

1.

2.

3.

4.

Answers: 1. Elephant, 2. Rat, 3. Owl, 4. Parrotfish

22

Rat poo is small. Sometimes rats eat their own poo!

Parrotfish poo out sand because they eat a stony sea creature called coral.

Owl poo is called a pellet. You can find out what an owl ate by looking inside the pellet for bones!

Elephants poo out 75 to 300 pounds (34 to 136 kg) of waste a day!

Glossary

energy The power to do work

intestines Long tubes in the body where most nutrients are taken from food and where waste is passed through

minerals A type of nutrient the body needs; natural substances that do not come from living things

mucus A slimy substance made by the body

muscles Parts of the body that help us move

stomach The body part where food goes to be broken down

throat The body part that leads from the mouth and nose to the long tube that connects to the stomach

vitamins A type of nutrient the body needs; natural substances that come from living things

Index